A Kid's Guide to Kenya

Curious Kids Press • Palm Springs, CA
www.curiouskidspress.com

Jack L. Roberts
Michael Owens

Photo: *A herd of buffalo in Kenya.*

A WORD TO PARENTS

CURIOUS KIDS PRESS is passionate about helping young readers expand and enhance their understanding about countries and cultures around the world. While actual real-world experiences with other countries and cultures may have the most profound positive effect on children and pre-teens, we understand such experiences are not always possible. That's why our two series of books — "A Kid's Guide to . . ." (for ages 9-12) and "Let's Visit . . ." (for ages 6-8) — are designed to bridge that gap and help young readers explore the wonderful world of diversity in everything from food and holidays to geography and traditions. We hope your young explorers enjoy this adventure into the awesome country of Kenya.

Publisher: Curious Kids Press, Palm Springs, CA 92264..
Editor: Sterling Moss
Designed by: Michael Owens
Copy Editor: Janice Ross

Copyright © 2017 by Curious Kids Press, LLC. All rights reserved. Except that any text portion of this book may be reproduced – mechanically, electronically, by hand or any other means you can think of – by any kid, anywhere, any time. For more information: info@curiouskidspress.com or 760-992-5962.

Table of Contents

Welcome to Kenya 4

Your Passport to Kenya.. 5

Where in the World Is Kenya.. 6

What Am I?... 7

A Brief History of Kenya... 8

5 Fun Facts About Kenya... 9

People, Customs, Culture..10

How to Speak Swahili..12

What's to Eat? The Food in Kenya... 13

Money, School, and Games... 14

Holidays in Kenya... 16

The Maasai: A Special Tribe of People.................................. 18

The Big 5... 22

The Elephant... 23

The Cape Buffalo.. 24

The Rhinoceros... 25

The Lion... 26

The Leopard.. 27

Glossary 28

For Parents and Teachers...32

Welcome to Kenya

"Jambo! Habari gani?"

IF YOU WANT TO SEE SOME AWESOME WILDLIFE, you've come to the right place. In the vast savanna of Kenya, there is an amazing variety of wildlife, like the two cheetahs pictured here, plus elephants, lions, giraffes, zebras, hippos, rhinos and much more. But Kenya is not just about the fantastic animals. It's also about the fantastic people. Meet any Kenyan for the first time. You're sure to get a big smile and a warm and friendly greeting. "Welcome," they'll say. Or, as they say in Swahili, "Karibu!"

Your Passport to Kenya

The Kenyan flag consists of four colors. Each color represents (or stands for) something. Black is for the people; red is for the struggle for freedom; green is for the fertile land; and white is for unity and peace. The shield and spears are traditional weapons of the Maasai people.

Kenya at a Glance
Official Name: Republic of Kenya
Capital City: Nairobi
Country Area (Size): 224,080 sq. miles (580,367 sq. km).
Population: 45,925,301 (By comparison, Texas and Florida together have about 46 million people.)
Official Language: Swahili (aka Kiswahili)

Where in the World Is Kenya?

KENYA IS A COUNTRY in Africa. It's about as big as Texas. The country is part of what is known as East Africa. Twenty African countries make up East Africa. Five of those East African countries border Kenya. Look at the map. Can you name the five countries that border Kenya?

Did You Know?

Kenya's motto is "Harambee." It means "Let us all pull together."

What Am I?
A Riddle

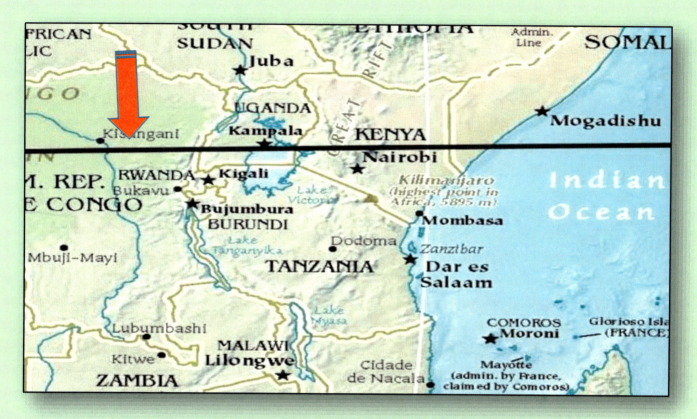

I'M TOTALLY IMAGINARY! But I'm also very important. I make it possible for people to navigate (or find) their way from one place to another around the world. I also divide the globe into two halves – the Northern Hemisphere and the Southern Hemisphere. What am I?

If you guessed "the equator," you're right. The equator passes through 13 countries. Kenya is one. Part of Kenya lies on in the Northern Hemisphere, and part of the country lies in the Southern Hemisphere. Can you find out what other countries lie in both the Northern and Southern Hemispheres?

A Brief History of Kenya

500 B.C. – 1000 A.D. Bantu-speaking people migrate from West Africa and Central Africa to what is now known as Kenya.

1498: Portuguese explorer Vasco de Gama reaches Kenya. For the next 100 years, Portuguese settlers try to take control of the coastal regions.

1830-1880: Many Kenyans are kidnapped and taken as slaves by Arabs, Europeans, and Americans.

1895: Britain takes over Kenya. It becomes known as British East Africa. Africans, however, are not allowed to participate in the government.

1920: Kenya becomes a British colony.

1952 - 1959: The "Mau Mau," a secret society, fights for independence from British control.

1963: Kenya wins independence from the United Kingdom; the Republic of Kenya is established.

2004: A devastating drought in Kenya causes a severe shortage of food; another drought occurs in 2006.

2010: A new constitution goes into effect. It limits the powers of the President.

2015: President Barack Obama visits Kenya, where his father was born.

5 Fun Facts About Kenya

1. Every year, more than 2 million wildebeest, zebra, and antelope migrate (or move) from the Serengeti National Park in Tanzania to the Maasai Mara National Reserve in Kenya and back again, a journey of 1,800 miles (2,896 km).

2. Kenya has only two seasons: one rainy season and one dry season.

3. Dennis Kimetto of Kenya holds the world record for a marathon (as of 2016): 2 hours, 2 minutes, and 57 seconds. The previous record holder was also from Kenya.

4. The two official languages in Kenya are Swahili (aka Kiswahili) and English; dozens of other little-known languages are also spoken.

5. The Sheldrick Elephant Orphanage, outside Nairobi, looks after orphan elephants and rhinos, so they can return to the wild.

The Best of Kenya: People, Customs, Culture

KENYA IS A BEAUTIFUL COUNTRY. It has gorgeous beaches and amazing wildlife parks and **reserves**.

Nairobi, the capital of Kenya, is a major **metropolitan** city with high-rise apartment buildings, shopping malls, night clubs, and a 60,000-seat sports stadium.

Yet, there is also a lot of poverty in Kenya. In Nairobi, more than half of all people there live in slums. Often, the small homes have no electricity or running water.

There are more than 40 different **ethnic** groups in Kenya –from the popular Maasai (see page 18) to the Kikuyu, who make up 20 percent of the nation's total population.

The people of Kenya are generally warm and friendly. That's why many people throughout the world call Kenya the "Jewel of Africa."

Background Photo: *Giraffe with Nairobi in the background.*

Kenya is a strange mixture of wealthy cities like Nairobi...

...and extremely poor villages.

The Nairobi National Park is located only 4 miles (7 km) from downtown Nairobi, where Kenya's wild animals are separated from the city by an electric fence.

How to Speak Swahili

Hello
Jambo
(JAHM-boh)

How are you?/ What's new?
Habari?
(huh-BAH-ree)

What's your name?
(Unaitwa nani?
OO-nah-EET-wah NAH-nee)

Cool
Poa!
(POH-ah)

My name is _____.
Jina langu ni _____.
(JEE-nah LAHN-goo nee _____.)

Thank you.
Asante
(ah-SAHN-teh)

Goodbye
Kwaheri
kwah-HAIR-ree

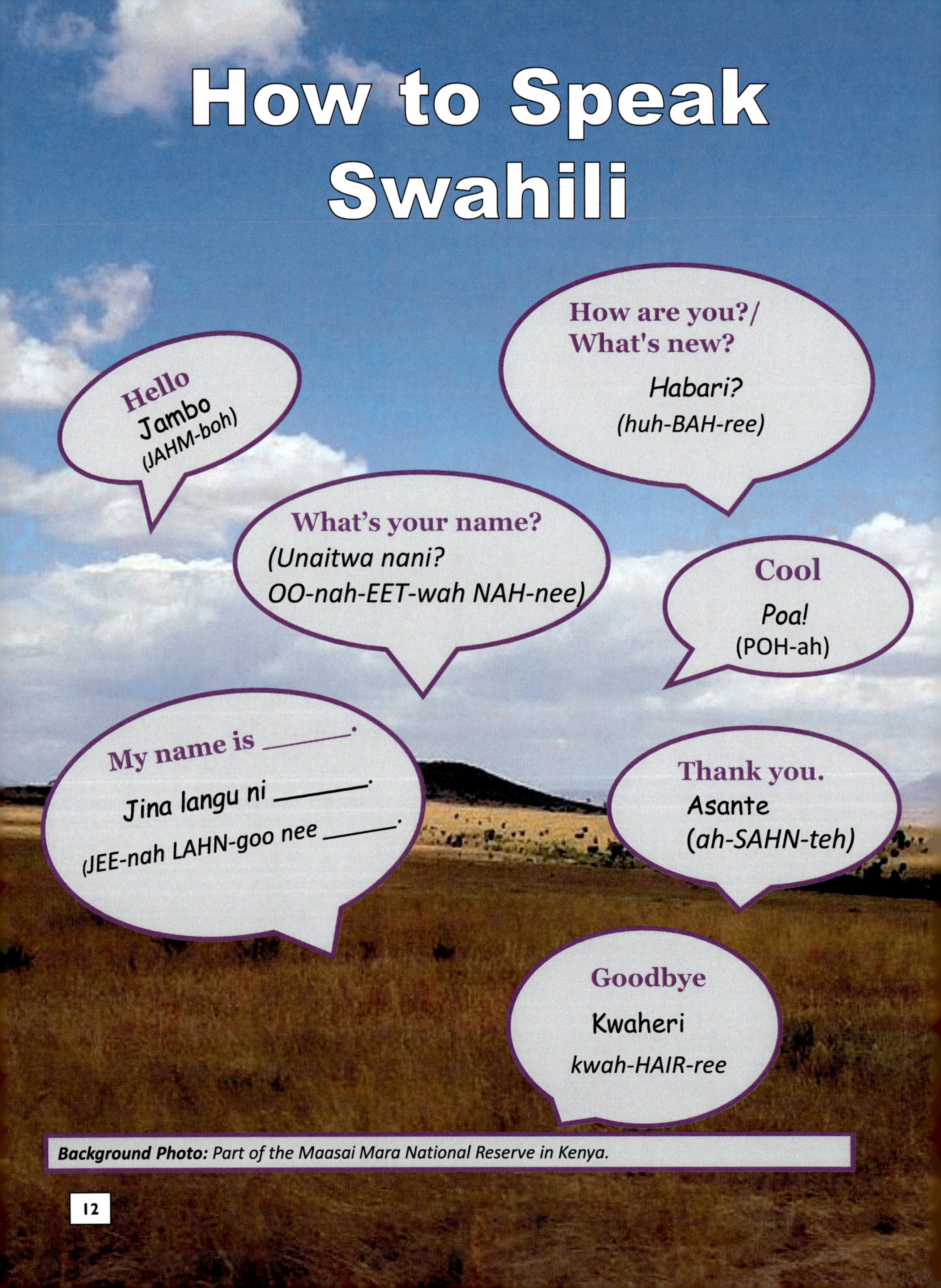

Background Photo: Part of the Maasai Mara National Reserve in Kenya.

What's to Eat? The Food in Kenya

WHAT'S YOUR FAVORITE FOOD? Chances are you'll find it in Kenya – everything from pizza to Kenya's answer to KFC – *Chicken Licken*. But if you want to try true Kenyan food, start with *ugali*. You'll find it everywhere – from fancy restaurants to street vendors. You can even use it to scoop up other dishes – no utensils necessary.

Breakfast
Mandazi: Fried dough in the shape of a donut.
Tea with milk

Lunch
Ugali: Cornmeal cooked with water into a cornmeal paste. Very thick and very heavy.

Snack
Chapatis: Kind of like fried flatbread.
Hot roasted maize: Grilled corn. (It can be found on the streets throughout Kenya.)

Dinner
Maharagwe: A bean stew in a coconut curry soup (often served with ugali).
Or
Nyama choma (Swahili for "roasted meat"): Kenya's unofficial national dish. Chunks of meat, potatoes, carrots, and other small vegetables.

If none of that sounds appetizing, you can always head over to Nairobi's Burger Hut restaurant for the best juicy burger in town.

Money, School, and Games

IN 2003, THE KENYA GOVERNMENT made public education free to all Kenyan children. But often young children are too busy to go to school. They must help their families earn a living by working the land or tending to cattle. When kids do go to school, the classroom is often overcrowded. They usually do not have computers or other electronic devices.

The money used in Kenya is called the Kenya shilling. In Swahili it's called *shilingi ya Kenya*. Current Kenyan banknotes feature the portrait of Jomo Kenyatta, Kenya's first president. The banknotes range in the denominations 50, 100, 200, 500 and 1,000 shillings.

An older 20 shilling note features Daniel arap Moi, the president of Kenya from 1978 to 2002.

Games Kids Play

KIDS IN KENYA, LIKE KIDS ALL OVER THE WORLD, have many games that they play. One of the favorite games in Kenya is call "Nyama, Nyama." (Nyama means "meat" in Swahili.)

In some ways, the "Nyama, Nyama" is like "Simon Says" that kids in America often play. The kids stand in a circle with one person in the middle. The person in the middle calls out the name of an animal. If it is an animal that is eaten for food, the children in the circle yell "Nyama, Nyama," as they jump up and down with their arms straight down by their sides. If the animal is not eaten for food, the children stand still and make no sound. If a player accidentally shouts or jumps, he or she must leave the game.

To see a YouTube video of kids having playing Nyama, Nyama, go to: https://www.youtube.com/watch?v=_tpa6FjHObw

Holidays in Kenya

KENYA CELEBRATES MANY OF THE SAME HOLIDAYS as the United States, including New Year's Day, Easter, and Christmas. But there are also some special holidays in Kenya as well. Here are three of them.

> **1. Madaraka Day (**June 1): On this day in 1963, Kenya attained internal self-rule. It took until December 1963, however, for the country to achieve total independence from the United Kingdom.

> **2. Mashujaa Day** (October 20): This holiday is also known as **Heroes' Day.** (*Mashujaa* in Swahili means *heroes*.) It honors all the men and women who contributed toward the struggle for Kenya's independence.

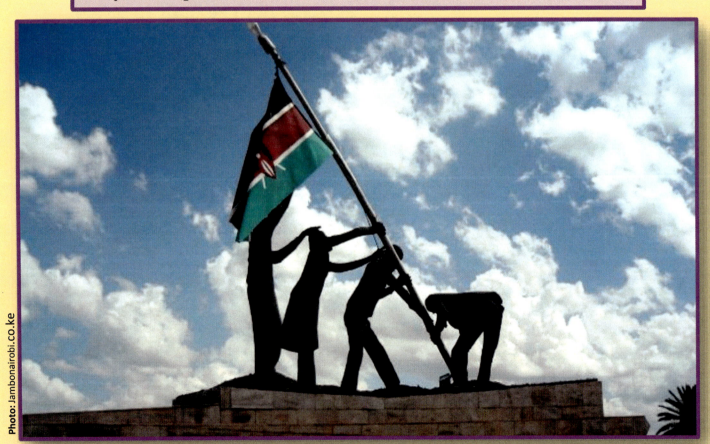

Kenya's struggle for independence is commemorated (or remembered) in this statue of freedom fighters raising the Kenya flag in Uhuru Gardens near Nairobi. (*Uhuru* means "freedom" in Swahili.)

Photo: Jambonairobi.co.ke

Holidays in Kenya

3. Jamhuri Day (December 12): *Jamhuri* is the Swahili word for "republic." The holiday marks the day when Kenya was established as a republic in 1964. Like the 4th of July in the United States, Jamhuri Day is celebrated with parades and dancing in the streets.

Dancers in Kenya perform during Jamhuri Day.

The Maasai
A Special Tribe of People in Kenya

A SAFARI IN KENYA is one of the most exciting adventures anyone could ever experience. But there is another adventure in Kenya that is equally amazing. It's a visit to a Maasai village (or *enkang*).

The Maasai (also spelled Masai, pronounced MAH-sigh) are a special and unique tribe of people in Kenya. They live mostly on the border between Kenya and Tanzania. They are **nomads**. That means that they travel from place to place.

The Maasai

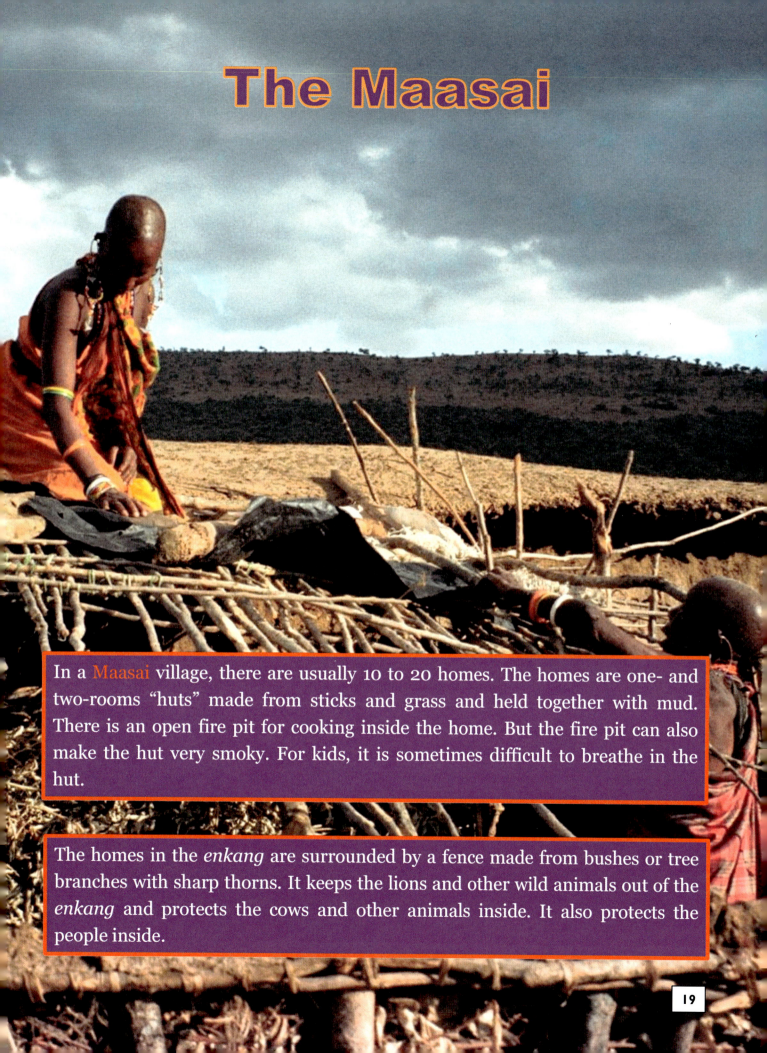

In a Maasai village, there are usually 10 to 20 homes. The homes are one- and two-rooms "huts" made from sticks and grass and held together with mud. There is an open fire pit for cooking inside the home. But the fire pit can also make the hut very smoky. For kids, it is sometimes difficult to breathe in the hut.

The homes in the *enkang* are surrounded by a fence made from bushes or tree branches with sharp thorns. It keeps the lions and other wild animals out of the *enkang* and protects the cows and other animals inside. It also protects the people inside.

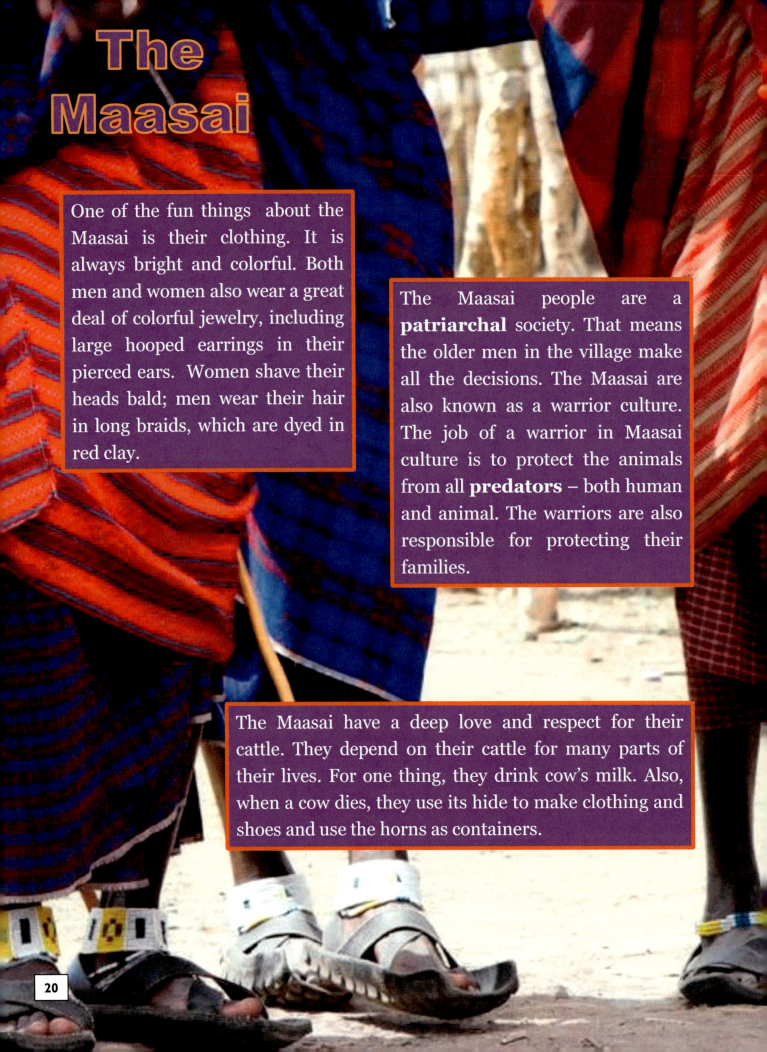

The Maasai

One of the fun things about the Maasai is their clothing. It is always bright and colorful. Both men and women also wear a great deal of colorful jewelry, including large hooped earrings in their pierced ears. Women shave their heads bald; men wear their hair in long braids, which are dyed in red clay.

The Maasai people are a **patriarchal** society. That means the older men in the village make all the decisions. The Maasai are also known as a warrior culture. The job of a warrior in Maasai culture is to protect the animals from all **predators** – both human and animal. The warriors are also responsible for protecting their families.

The Maasai have a deep love and respect for their cattle. They depend on their cattle for many parts of their lives. For one thing, they drink cow's milk. Also, when a cow dies, they use its hide to make clothing and shoes and use the horns as containers.

The Maasai

The young Maasai warriors (called *morani*) have many fascinating traditions and rituals. One ritual is called the Jumping Dance. It takes place during a boy's transition into manhood, called *eunoto*.

The warriors form a circle. One at a time, the morani enter the circle. They jump straight up without letting the heels of their feet touch the ground. Young women watch carefully. The best jumper – the one who jumps the highest and is most graceful – is chosen as chief of the group. He is also the one the girls want to be with.

The Big 5

KENYA IS FAMOUS FOR ITS WILDLIFE. It's the home of lions, elephants, zebras, giraffes, rhinoceros, warthogs, wildebeests, and other fascinating wild animals. There are also over 1,000 kinds of birds in Kenya.

Thousands of visitors travel to Kenya each year to go on a safari (a Swahili word for "journey") to see these amazing animals.

The most famous of Kenya's wild animals are known as "The Big 5" (see picture below). They are the animals that tourists usually want to see the most.

In Africa, the Big 5 game animals are (from left to right) the African elephant, the Cape buffalo, the rhinoceros, the African lion, and the African leopard.

How "the big 5" got its name

Many years ago, big game hunters came up with the term. They felt those five animals were the most difficult to hunt on foot. Today, fortunately, most big game hunters are *hunting with cameras*, not guns.

The African Elephant

Did You Know?

Like a newborn baby sucking its thumb, a newborn elephant (called a **calf**) often sucks its trunk for comfort.

THE AFRICAN ELEPHANT is the largest mammal in the world. It stands up to 14 ft (4.2 m) tall and is 30 ft (9.1 m) wide. It weighs up to 12,000 pounds (5,443 kg). Yet, it is one of the most affectionate and social animals in Kenya.

For years, elephants were hunted and killed for their ivory tusks. But, today, there is a ***ban worldwide on the sale of ivory***. That ban has helped save the population of elephants around the world.

The Cape Buffalo

Did You Know?

Buffalo are very good swimmers and often cross deep water in search of better grazing.

HERE'S A SURPRISING FACT: The Cape Buffalo is said to have killed more Big Game Hunters over the years than any other animal in Africa. The good news is if you leave them alone (we will), they are quite peaceful. Adult males can grow to be 6 ft (1.8 m) tall and weigh 1,500 pounds (700 kg).

The Rhinoceros

Did You Know?

Despite its large size, the black rhino is quite nimble (or graceful in its movements) and can make sharp turns even while running at full speed – 30 mph (48 km/h).

THE BLACK AFRICAN RHINO and the white African rhino are neither black or white – they're both gray! But that's not all that's surprising about these magnificent animals. You can tell the difference between a black rhino and a white rhino by its lips. The black rhino has a strange upper lip that can grasp leaves and twigs. It's called a prehensile lip. A white rhino has a long flat lip that it uses for grazing. By an elephant's standard, the rhino is rather small. It weighs only about half of what an elephant weighs.

The Lion

Did You Know?

When African lions roar, their sound can be heard as far as 5 miles (8 km) away.

THE AFRICAN LION is known as the king of the jungle. That's strange, since the lion doesn't actually live in a jungle at all! It lives in the open **savanna** where it hunts other wild animals like the antelope and zebra.

Unlike other cats in Kenya and other parts of Africa, the African lion is social and lives in a pride. The pride consists of several females, their children, and a couple of males. So why is it called the king of the jungle? Maybe it's because of its enormous power and strength – and, some might say, its stunning beauty.

The Leopard

Did You Know?

The leopard's spots are circular in East Africa, but square in southern Africa.

WOULD YOU LIKE to see an African leopard on your next safari? Then, look up. Leopards like to hide in trees – not only for protection, but to watch for possible food sources. The African Leopard is a shy animal even though leopards can weigh as much as 200 pounds (92 kg). They are also great runners and pretty good swimmers. And they can jump! Boy, can they jump – as high as 10 feet (3 m) straight up! The leopard's spots help to camouflage it from its only predators who are – sad to say – human beings.

Glossary

Calf — The young of cattle and other mammals, such as whales or elephants.

Camouflage — A method of hiding something by covering it or coloring so as to imitate its surroundings.

Colony — A territory governed by a distant country.

Diverse — Of various types or sorts; assorted.

Ethnic — Of or related to a large group of people who share the same culture, language, and customs.

Metropolitan — Of or pertaining to a major city; urban.

Paleontology — The scientific study of life in the past through examination of fossils.

Patriarchal — Having to do with the elderly male leader of a family or tribe.

Predator — An animal that hunts other animals for food.

Prey — An animal being hunted, caught, and eaten by another animal.

Ritual — A series of steps or actions often done in a religious or other ceremony.

Safari — A journey, trip, or expedition for watching or hunting large animals.

Savanna — A flat plain covered with grass and a few trees, found in Africa.

Hope you enjoyed reading this book about Kenya.

Come visit us sometime.

Explore the World

Find these books on Amazon.com
Preview them at curiouskidspress.com

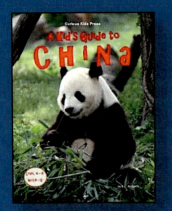
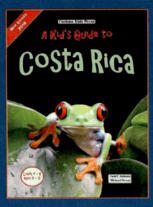
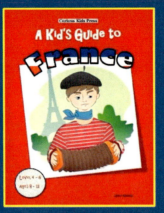
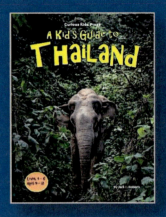
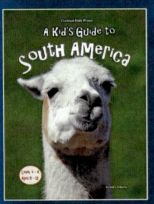

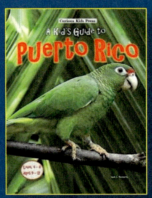
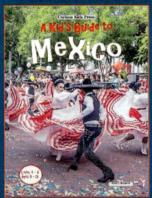
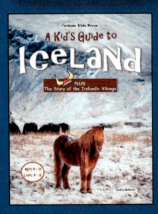

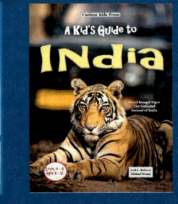
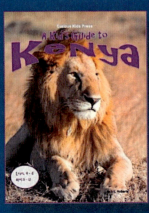
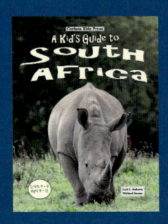
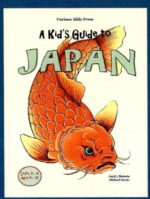
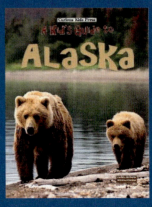

Curious Kids Press
www.curiouskidspress.com

Two important new books for all young readers and their families.

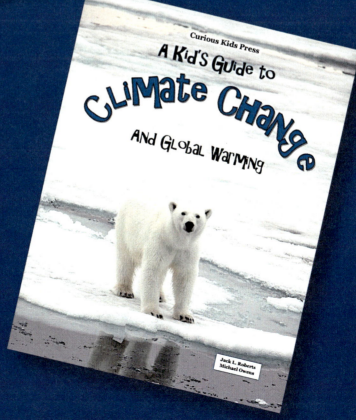

Available on amazon.com

A Kid's Guide to
Kenya
For Parents and Teachers

About This Book

A Kid's Guide to . . . is an engaging, easy-to-read book series that provides an exciting adventure into fascinating countries and cultures around the world for young readers. Each book focuses on one country, continent, or U.S. territory or state, and includes colorful photographs, informational charts and graphs, and quirky and bizarre "Did You Know" facts, all designed to bring the country and its people to life. Designed primarily for recreational, high-interest reading, the informational text series is also a great resource for students to use to research geography topics or writing assignments.

About the Reading Level

A Kid's Guide to . . . is an informational text series designed for kids in grades 4 to 6, ages 9 to 12. For some young readers, the series will provide new reading challenges based on the vocabulary and sentence structure. For other readers, the series will review and reinforce reading skills already achieved. While for still other readers, the book will match their current skill level, regardless of age or grade level.

About the Authors

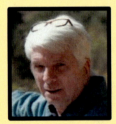

Jack L. Roberts began his career in educational publishing at Children's Television Workshop (now Sesame Workshop), where he was Senior Editor of The Sesame Street/Electric Company Reading Kits. Later, at Scholastic Inc., he was the founding editor of a high-interest/low-reading level magazine for middle school students. He also founded two technology magazines for teachers and administrators.

Roberts is the author of more than two dozen biographies and other nonfiction titles for young readers, published by Scholastic Inc., the Lerner Publishing Group, Teacher Created Materials, Benchmark Education, and others.. More recently, he was the co-founder of WordTeasers, an educational series of card decks designed to help kids of all ages improve their vocabulary through "conversation, not memorization."

Michael Owens is a noted jazz dance teacher, award-winning wildlife photographer, graphic arts designer, and devoted animal lover.

In 2017, Roberts and Owens launched Curious Kids Press (CKP), an educational publishing company focused on publishing high-interest, nonfiction books for young readers, primarily books about countries and cultures around the world. Currently, CKP has published two series of country books: "A Kid's Guide to..." (for ages 9-12 and "Let's Visit . . ." (for ages 6-8) — both designed to help young readers explore the wonderful world of diversity in everything from food and holidays to geography and traditions.

To Our Valued Customers

Curious Kids Press is passionate about creating fun-to-read books about countries and cultures around the world for young readers, and we work hard every day to create quality products.

All of our books are Print on Demand books. As a result, on rare occasions, you may find minor printing errors. If you feel you have not received a quality printed product, please send us a description and photo of the printing error along with your name and address and we will have a new copy sent to you free of charge. Contact us at: info@curiouskidspress.com

Made in the USA
Coppell, TX
18 December 2021